PIANO | VOCAL | GUITAR

MELISSA ETHERIDGE
GREATEST HITS | THE ROAD LESS TRAVELED

ISBN 1-4234-0579-X

HAL•LEONARD® CORPORATION

7777 W. BLUEMOUND RD. P.O. BOX 13819 MILWAUKEE, WI 53213

Visit Hal Leonard Online at
www.halleonard.com

CONTENTS

Due to licensing restrictions, "Breathe" is not included in this publication.

REFUGEE

Words and Music by TOM PETTY
and MIKE CAMPBELL

SIMILAR FEATURES

Words and Music by
MELISSA ETHERIDGE

Medium beat

Go on and close your eyes, go on i - mag - ine me there. She's got

sim - i - lar fea - tures, with long - er hair. And if that's what it takes to

LIKE THE WAY I DO

Words and Music by
MELISSA ETHERIDGE

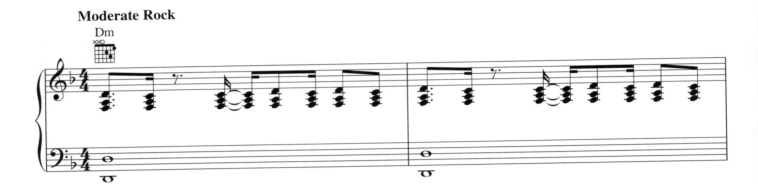

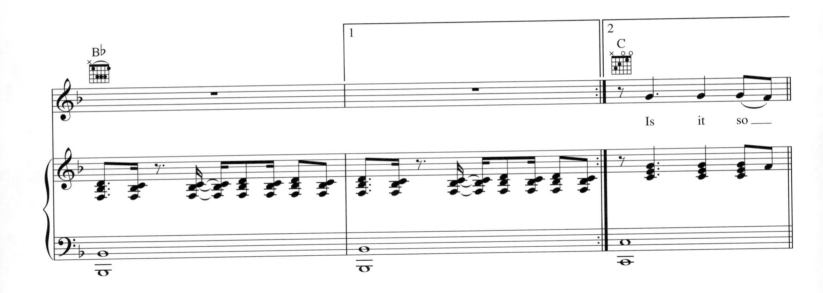

15

BRING ME SOME WATER

Words and Music by
MELISSA ETHERIDGE

To-night I feel so weak,
When will this ach-ing pass?

but all in love is _____ fair.
When will this night be _____ through?

I turn the oth-er cheek,
I want to hear the break-ing glass.

ba - by's got my mind. But to - night the sweet dev - il,

sweet dev - il's got my soul.

soul.

molto rit.

YOU CAN SLEEP WHILE I DRIVE

Words and Music by
MELISSA ETHERIDGE

Moderately

Come on, ba - by, let's get out of this town. I got a

full tank of gas — with the top rolled down. — There's a chill in my bones, — I don't want to

be left a - lone, — so, ba - by, you can sleep while — I drive. —

NO SOUVENIRS

Words and Music by
MELISSA ETHERIDGE

Moderate Rock

Hel - lo, hel - lo.___
Once, twice,___
This is Ro - me - o___
I thought it might be nice___

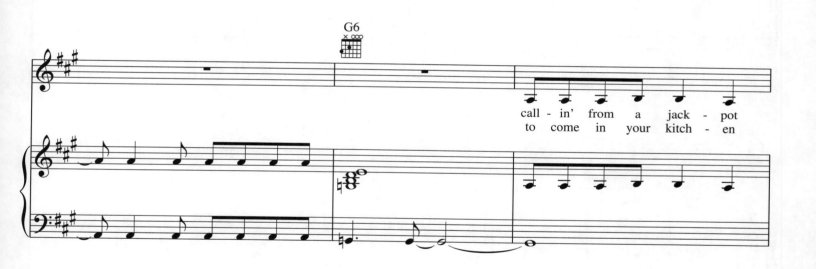

call - in' from a jack - pot
to come in your kitch - en

tel - e - phone.
and play.
Shame, shame,___
Cool, cool,___

D.S. al Coda

You don't wan-na know where I'm call-in' you from, or how come.

CODA

with no sou - ve - nirs. _____ *Vocal 1st time only*

lo, hel - lo. _____ This is Ro - me - o. _____

Hel -

AIN'T IT HEAVY

Words and Music by
MELISSA ETHERIDGE

Some - times_ I know that it's nev - er e - nough._ Sur -
in' kind - a loose,_ I'm feel - in' kind - a mean; I've been

36

Heav - y, ain't it heav - y. Ain't the night heav - y.

I'm feel -

I'M THE ONLY ONE

Words and Music by
MELISSA ETHERIDGE

Please, ba - by, can't_ you see my
Please, ba - by, can't_ you see I'm

mind's a burn - in' hell. _ I got ra - zors a - rip - pin' and tear - in', and strip - in' my
try - in' to ex - plain. _ I've been here be - fore and I'm lock - in' the door and I'm

heart a - part as well.
not go - in' back a - gain. __

To - night you told me that you
Her eyes and arms and skin won't

ache for some - thing new, __
make it go a - way. __

and some oth - er wom - an is look - in' like some - thing that
You'll wake up to - mor - row and wres - tle the sor - row that

Am

might be good for you. }
holds you down to - day. }

Go on and hold her till the

D

Am

scream - in' is gone. __

Go on, be - lieve her when she

COME TO MY WINDOW

Words and Music by
MELISSA ETHERIDGE

IF I WANTED TO

Words and Music by
MELISSA ETHERIDGE

Oh, — oh. — Oh, — oh. — Oh, — oh. —

Oh, — oh. — If I want-ed to, I could do an-
want-ed to, I could run fast —

-y-thing right. I could dance with the dev-il on a Sat-ur-day — night. — If I
— as a train, be as sharp as a nee-dle — that's twist-ing your — brain. — If I

56

I WANT TO COME OVER

Words and Music by
MELISSA ETHERIDGE

I know you're home; _____

you left your light _____
you told her a - bout
I know that you're shak -

_____ on.
_____ me.
- en.

You know I'm _____ here; _____
She filled you with _____ fear, _____
You think we'll be _____ lost _____

*Vocals written one octave higher than sung.

66

to see ___ you a - gain. ___

(Vocal 1st time only)

Repeat and Fade

Optional Ending

ANGELS WOULD FALL

Words and Music by MELISSA ETHERIDGE
and JOHN SHANKS

CODA II

An - gels __ would __

fall. __

Vocal 1st time only

Repeat and Fade | Optional Ending

LUCKY

Words and Music by
MELISSA ETHERIDGE

Moderately fast

I wan-na see __ how luck-y

luck-y can be,

yeah.

split the ac - es to the rac - es, I feel luck-y to-night.

D.S. al Coda

CHRISTMAS IN AMERICA

Words and Music by
MELISSA ETHERIDGE

* Vocal written one octave higher than sung.

PIECE OF MY HEART

Words and Music by BERT BERNS
and JERRY RAGOVOY

come ___ on, come ___ on, come ___ on, come ___ on.

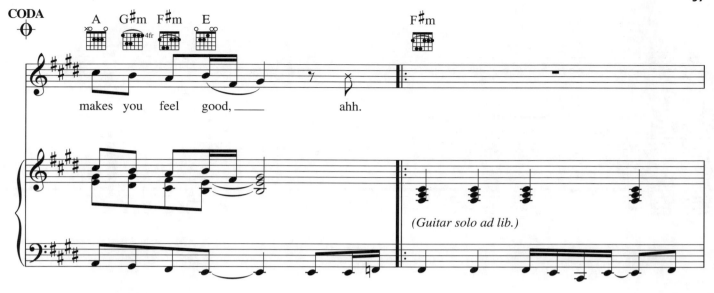

makes you feel good, ____ ahh.

(Guitar solo ad lib.)

Play 3 times

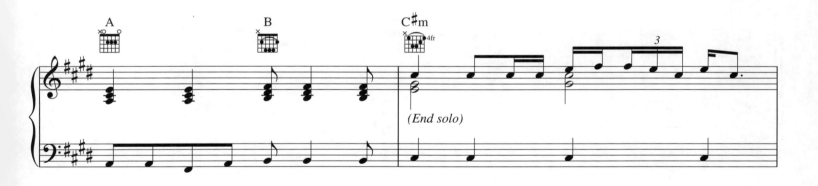

(End solo)

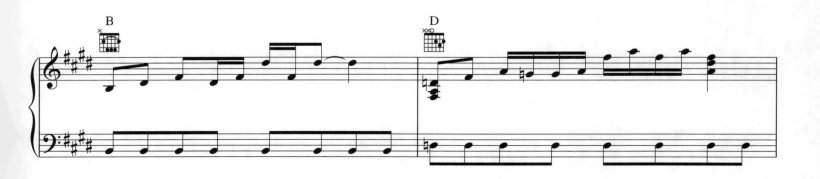

THIS IS NOT GOODBYE

Words and Music by
MELISSA ETHERIDGE

Moderately slow, with feeling

Brave - ly you let go of my hand.

I can't speak yet you un - der - stand.

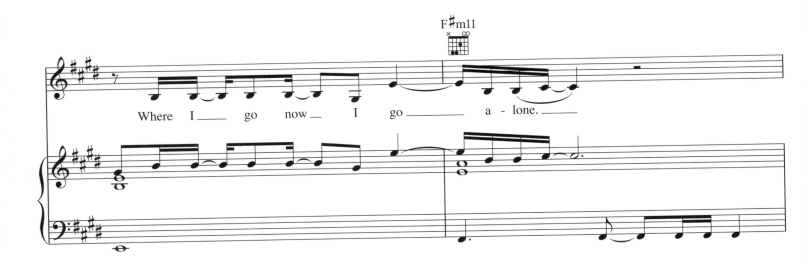

Where I go now I go a - lone.

Wait for __ me here. __

Si - lent - ly stay __ and don't ask me why. __

On - ly __ be - lieve __

this is not good - bye. __

I RUN FOR LIFE

Words and Music by
MELISSA ETHERIDGE

Moderately fast

E5
B5
moth - er, your sis - ter, your wife. I run for
C♯5
4fr
B5
To Coda
A5
5fr
you and me, my friend. I run for life.
E5
It's a
E
F♯m11
blur since they told me a - bout it, how the